THE
PISCES
ORACLE

THE
PISCES
ORACLE

INSTANT ANSWERS FROM
YOUR COSMIC SELF

STELLA FONTAINE

greenfinch

Introduction

Welcome to your zodiac oracle, carefully crafted especially for you Pisces, and brimming with the wisdom of the universe.

Is there a tricky-to-answer question niggling at you and you need an answer?

Whenever you're unsure whether to say 'yes' or 'no', whether to go back or to carry on, whether to trust or to turn away, make some time for a personal session with your very own oracle. Drawing on your astrological profile, your zodiac oracle will guide you in understanding, interpreting and answering those burning questions that life throws your way. Discovering your true path will become an enlightening journey of self-actualization.

Humans have long cast their eyes heavenwards to seek answers from the universe. For millennia the sun, moon and stars have been our constant companions as they repeat their paths and patterns across the skies. We continue to turn to the cosmos for guidance, trusting in the deep and abiding wisdom of the universe as we strive for fulfilment, truth and understanding.

The most basic and familiar aspect of astrology draws on the twelve signs of the zodiac, each connected to a unique constellation as well as its own particular colours, numbers and characteristics. These twelve familiar signs are also known as the sun signs: Aries, Taurus, Gemini, Cancer, Leo, Virgo, Libra, Scorpio, Sagittarius, Capricorn, Aquarius and Pisces.

Aries Taurus Gemini Cancer Leo Virgo

Libra Scorpio Sagittarius Capricorn Aquarius Pisces

Each sign is associated with an element (fire, air, earth or water), and also carries a particular quality: cardinal (action-takers), fixed (steady and constant) and mutable (changeable and transformational). Beginning to understand these complex combinations, and to recognize the layered influences they bring to bear on your life, will unlock your own potential for personal insight, self-awareness and discovery.

In our data-flooded lives, now more than ever it can be difficult to know where to turn for guidance and advice. With your astrology oracle always by your side, navigating life's twists and turns will become a smoother, more mindful process. Harness the prescience of the stars and tune in to the resonance of your sun sign with this wisdom-packed guide that will lead you to greater self-knowledge and deeper confidence in the decisions you are making. Of course, not all questions are created equal; your unique character, your circumstances and the issues with which you find yourself confronted all add up to a conundrum unlike any other... but with your question in mind and your zodiac oracle in your hand, you're already halfway to the answer.

Pisces
FEBRUARY 19 TO MARCH 20

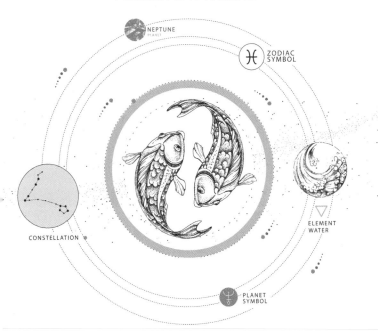

Element: Water

Quality: Mutable

Named for the constellation: Pisces (the fish)

Ruled by: Neptune

Opposite: Virgo

Characterized by: Intuition, gentleness, romance

Colours: Purples, green

How to Use This Book

You can engage with your oracle whenever you need to but, for best results, create an atmosphere of calm and quiet, somewhere you will not be disturbed, making a place for yourself and your question to take priority. Whether this is a particular physical area you turn to in times of contemplation, or whether you need to fence off a dedicated space within yourself during your busy day, that all depends on you and your circumstances. Whichever you choose, it is essential that you actively put other thoughts and distractions to one side in order to concentrate upon the question you wish to answer.

Find a comfortable position, cradle this book lightly in your hands, close your eyes, centre yourself. Focus on the question you wish to ask. Set your intention gently and mindfully towards your desire to answer this question, to the exclusion of all other thoughts and mind-chatter. Allow all else to float softly away, as you remain quiet and still, gently watching the shape and form of the question you wish to address. Gently deepen and slow your breathing.

Tune in to the ancient resonance of your star sign, the vibrations of your surroundings, the beat of your heart and the flow of life and the universe moving in and around you. You are one with the universe.

Now simply press the book between your palms as you clearly and distinctly ask your question (whether aloud or in your head), then open it at any page. Open your eyes. Your advice will be revealed.

Read it carefully. Take your time turning this wisdom over in your mind, allowing your thoughts to surround it, to absorb it, flow with it, then to linger and settle where they will.

Remember, your oracle will not provide anything as blunt and brutal as a completely literal answer. That is not its role. Rather, you will be gently guided towards the truth you seek through your own consciousness, experience and understanding. And as a result, you will grow, learn and flourish.

Let's begin.

Close your eyes.

Hold the question you want
answered clearly in your mind.

Open your oracle to any page to
reveal your cosmic insight.

When in doubt Pisces, take it
to the water every time. Bath, shower,
swim, walk in the rain – you'll be in
your element and all will become clear.

Your pure Piscean instincts
for equanimity, graciousness and
generosity often shape themselves
into the gift of excellent advice. But
lean into your intuition this time and
keep it to yourself. As well-meant
as they are, there is a chance
your words may be taken as
unwelcome criticism.

When you know what it is you really want, there is nothing more attractive than that kind and gentle empathy Pisces is so famous for.

Your answer lies directly in front
of you; do the thing you are surest you
won't regret later on. That will be best.

Time to harness all the magical
parts of your Pisces nature to cope
with this one. Draw your energy
upwards. Address the situation.
Make it count.

Although it feels you have come a long way already, you are still not at the end of your journey.

Continue to work on relationships, particularly with friends and family. In many ways this is a life's work, but it will also bring a lifetime of rewards. Move forwards with care, patience and loving kindness.

Taking care of yourself must be
your priority; with Neptune in charge,
a little rest, solitude and perhaps even
some spiritual work might be just
what you need.

Stories hold some clues and insight that you have been craving Pisces. Read a book, watch a film and open your heart to welcome the wisdom you find within.

Stimulating conversation may result from a chance meeting, whether in person or virtual. Is this what you have been missing?

There is a beautiful release in relinquishing control and it is time to show faith in your star-path. You do not need to have all the answers, your direction ahead is already illuminated. Believe, let go and follow.

It is perhaps time to alter your course in dealing with this one, there is a chance you might have taken the wrong tack at first. Best to reset your compass and view this as a chance to learn and move forwards.

If you sense things shifting beneath the surface right now, take some time to examine the likely causes.

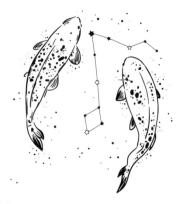

Your malleable and adaptable
nature means that you are sometimes
overlooked Pisces; perhaps others are
uncertain of your contribution. Don't
miss the opportunity to own your
achievements this time.

With Virgo as your opposite
sign, sometimes you need to cool
that spark and engage with a little
more watchfulness and clarity.
Now is one of those times.

There is potential for
misunderstanding in communications
at the moment. Do not risk causing
offense and upset, keep your thoughts
to yourself and enjoy the calm.

Careful, calm and compassionate, you are quick to surround yourself with like-minded people. You definitely benefit from their wisdom and willingness to do the hard work. Of course, they love you, but you should make sure they know that you appreciate them, too.

You pride yourself on the care
and love with which you nurture
your relationships, and infinitely prefer
to avoid drama and antagonism. You
need not engage with this one; just
watch and wait. It will resolve itself
without your intervention.

Your success on this occasion
will hinge on your ability to engage
with patience and persistence. You
are skilled at both of those.
Bide your time.

Despite your unfailingly generous nature and preference for gentle encouragement, this might be one of those situations in which actions speak louder than words. Quiet your voice and busy yourself with activity instead.

As tempting as it is to ask the safe questions, are you sure this is the one you really want an answer to? Give it some thought, re-frame and try again.

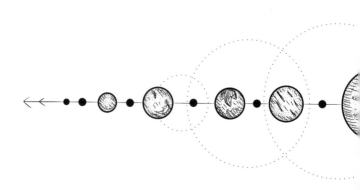

Your integrity is everything to you
and it is essential you stay true to your
personal commitments; you won't feel
easy with yourself if you don't.

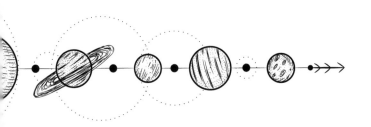

Empathy and compassion in
all things Pisces, it is written in your
stars. Your generosity and intuition
will guide you through.

You should be proud of the
high regard in which others hold
you Pisces, it is well-deserved. But
protecting it should not be at the cost
of your happiness. Follow your heart
and the rest will fall into place.

Endeavour to remain open to the possibilities that lie ahead. Change is on your horizon, but there is nothing you can do to plan for it. Be ready.

Warmly supportive relationships
are one of life's purest pleasures for a
peace-loving Pisces, but don't forget
to support yourself as well as those
around you. Compromise
needn't mean cost.

You are usually so awake to
the needs of others that it will
be a surprise to think you may have
overlooked someone in this. Perhaps
you didn't even notice they were there,
wanting something, hoping to be seen.
Be extra alert to this possibility
right now.

Your intuitive understanding
and clear, selfless heart bring the
very best of relationships to your door
Pisces. But remember these attributes
can also attract the less-desirables; be
aware that part of your nature can
be inclined to trust too easily.

Do not underestimate yourself
Pisces – battering down the door is
not the only way to get what you
want. In gentleness and patience
lies ultimate strength.

You are known for your ability to balance a big-picture view with a carefully thought-through approach. But take advice where you need it, you can't possibly do it all by yourself.

Suspend judgement until you
have heard the whole story; your skill
in this is rare and infinitely valuable.
Exercise it now.

Consider this one further - your plan is carefully constructed, but it might be that it would benefit from a little more thought. Only you can know the truth on this occasion.

Your patience and loyalty
are particular Piscean gifts. You
are blessed among the star-signs
but remember that not everyone has
been quite so lucky. Envy might drive
others to disparage these beautiful
aspects of your character. Ignore
them and move on.

Neptune brings music, light, intuition, creativity and wisdom into your life, as well as opportunities for great joy. Be grateful for these gifts and generous.

The pressure you place on yourself to succeed may be adding to the weight your spirit is already lumbered with. This one is tricky, but probably not for the reasons you think. Lighten the load and you'll do better.

Pisces, it's time to show yourself some love. Turn some of that kindness you so generously bestow on those around you inwards.

This part is tough, but you are learning lessons for the future. What comes next is entirely in your hands. Learn from the past and move on.

Time to take a break from
that long-view plan Pisces, and
sink into the now.

You can seem mysterious,
perhaps even slippery, to others
Pisces. What you project is what they
will understand of you; they cannot
know what is in your heart unless
you tell them.

This is a slippery fish and the measurements are not precisely as they seemed at first glance. Take a closer look – there is detail there that was not apparent to start with.

Generous, gentle and genuine, it's easy to understand why others hold you in such high affection. Be careful to return the favour – you mustn't leave anyone feeling taken for granted, as that can easily go wrong.

This time you need to know that there is probably only one best outcome. It is not an occasion for spontaneity. Proceed with caution.

Context is everything;
nothing and no one stands alone
and circumstances are inextricably
linked to outcome.

Success will follow, but it may not be dressed quite as you had expected. Hold the door open to all possibilities. A series of small wins is the key to this one; acknowledge each as you go.

You will be best placed
to make this important verdict
if you tune in to your inner voice
Pisces. Failing to heed your
intuition would be a mistake.

Gifted with empathy
and a keen eye for the struggles
of others, it is important you do not
absorb too much of their story or
sadness into your own soul. Keep it
light Pisces, you must
stay afloat.

Others are gently drawn to you;
now it's time to make the most of
your Piscean talents to pull the
right people together.

Harmony and calm really
resonate with you, and you
will do almost anything to avoid
unpleasant situations. But remember,
out of sight does not always mean
out of mind, much as you
would like it to.

You flow like the water sign you
are, easy and accommodating, almost
shape-shifting around awkward
obstacles. But remember it is
important to remind people what
you stand for occasionally.
Proceed accordingly.

Don't shy away from the
challenge; this is especially important
now. Nothing worth doing seems easy
at first, but you are more than
up to this one.

Step out of your comfort zone Pisces.
There are no challenges for you there.

Choose forgiveness
over judgement Pisces.

Your harmonious nature combines with a quiet determination, making you a true force. When decisive action is required, you are more than up to the task.

Gentle doesn't mean weak and
quiet self-belief is in steady supply
for you Pisces. Your careful approach
won't let you down. You have the deep
knowledge already within you to
make the right choice.

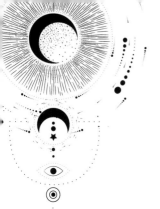

Careful is one thing, boring is another. Make sure this doesn't end up becoming so predictable that you (or they) lose interest. Open the weir a little bit. Raise the level.

You are not obsessed with success, at least not in the conventional sense, but nevertheless it is important to acknowledge your wins. Whether big or small, they are key to your life satisfaction. You should be proud of the way things are going.

You know the importance of flow better than anyone Pisces, but sometimes even you are tempted to hold on too tightly. Let go and allow things to be as they are. The knotty ones do have a way of eventually working themselves smooth again. And if they don't, they don't.

Time to recharge your soul
Pisces; essential maintenance for the
harmony you so love. Yoga, swimming,
sinking into music, taking a sound
bath, meditation, singing bowls –
these are all guaranteed to
soothe your spirit.

Clear-sighted as you are, sometimes a focused plan of attack can seem a little beyond you. Leave indecision at the door on your way in today; this time, choosing a direction and making a move are more important than waiting for a sign.

Others may find it difficult to
get a handle on who you really are
Pisces; given your watery nature, you
seem to flow through people's hands,
frustrating attempts to hold you in
one place. Make the most of this
today; after all, blocky concrete
solidity is not all it's cracked
up to be.

Flow is stronger than resistance.
If there is one thing you understand
better than most Pisces, it is that the
power of dynamism will triumph over
the static. Every. Single. Time.

Neptune, your ruling
planet, is the bringer of dreams,
illusion and other-worldliness. More
straightforward signs may find these
aspects of Pisces confusing, perhaps
even frustrating. But Neptune bestows
on you a higher level of inspiration,
purity and sensitivity than most. Make
good use of your visionary skills now.

Given your propensity for escapism, it may have taken you longer than most to decide what you want. But now you're clear (sort of), your Piscean intuition will guide you forwards. Allow it to happen.

Adversity often brings opportunity, and you are adept at finding the positives. See past the immediate issue to what likely lies ahead. You don't need to have a full plan in order to make a start.

Sensitivity, beauty and gentleness
are fundamental for you Pisces; they
bring the magic into your life. You are
happy to sacrifice for the greater good
or for those you love; just be mindful
not to lose yourself in the process.

Your innate innocence
(some might call it naivety, but
what do they know?) is a beautiful
characteristic common to those ruled
by Neptune. As is forgiveness. Spread
the love but don't allow others to take
advantage of your sweet nature.
You won't be doing them any
favours in the long run.

Easy flexibility and adaptability are essential for Pisces, so it can be disturbing when you are trapped within too much pressure. Trust that there is a greater plan at work right now. Breathe, stay in the moment, shimmy your way out from under anything (or anyone) seeking to hold you, and this too shall pass.

Time for a clean perspective Pisces. You know that there is a better way to go about this, despite the fact it may look a little more difficult from this angle. Don't allow yourself to be disheartened.

Pisces is a water sign, constantly striving to maintain the flow, and the deft lightness of your natural touch serves you well. On this occasion, keep your feet firmly planted to ensure you remain grounded and maintain your energy.

It is possible you may need some help with this one. Friends and family will be willing, but you must be clear about what you need from them.

It is all manageable, especially for you Pisces. But you might need to look at this one from a different angle. The direction of approach will make all the difference to your chances of success.

Escape to the water to give
yourself time and space for thinking
this one through; a change of scenery
will benefit your decision-making
process enormously.

Notice and allow. Acknowledge
the thinking part of your brain but
know that it is not necessary for you
to engage with it right now.
Balance and breathe.

Try to stay present and not drift into the misty-maybe imagination zone. You will need your wits about you to tackle this one.

It is essential to embrace the broad overview this time; luckily, you don't need to understand the workings of all those little cogs down there in the belly of the thing. To achieve that best-for-everyone outcome, rise above the detail and go with it.

Engage your star-given gift
for suspending judgement and
forgive the mistakes that have been
made, whether by you or by someone
else. Forgiving doesn't mean
forgetting but moving on is the
only practical solution here.

You can find it difficult to keep your feet on the ground but retaining that top-to-toe connection is important if you are to avoid drifting off altogether. Reflexology is a helpful treatment for you Pisces, or you could try simply taking a barefoot stroll along the beach or on the grass.

Throw that intuition into high
gear; possibility is more complex
and infinitely more beautiful than just
that which is visible on the surface.
But this you know already.

Loyalty, patience and generosity
are all hallmarks of your essential
Pisces-ness. But you will only keep
bringing your best self if you allow
your energy to replenish. Switch off
the screens and embrace some
downtime today; you'll be ready
to face the universe again in no time.

You must draw on those magical Piscean depths to pull up precisely the right question. Then ask it. All will be easy from there and the answer will reveal itself right in front of you.

Your Pisces instinct was, of course, correct. There was a reason something smelt a bit fishy. Follow your intuition on this one.

Don't be tempted to do this someone else's way, for whatever reason. The decision to aim for a system-shaking change is rarely made well as a knee-jerk reaction, and anyway that's not really your style. Sleep on it.

More often than not, the real world might seem overly harsh to a Pisces. But don't withdraw too far into a fantasy-mist simply to avoid it, and don't be tempted to sidestep your own integrity either. Illusions will not help you right now – it's important to see clearly.

Speaking your truth is
not always a guaranteed path to
cementing relationships, and anyway
it's all so subjective. If your opinion is
sought, counsel others to suspend
their judgements; if they must have
their say, they should consider
all likely outcomes first.

Abandon attachment and thoughts of control – neither will serve you on this occasion.

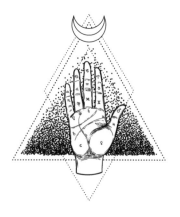

A true friend is one who tells you what you *need* to hear, rather than simply what you *want* to hear. Loyalty and truth go together on this one. Do not allow your ego to guide your response.

You cannot control the
outcome, so release any feelings
of responsibility or accountability.
Make the coolest, cleanest decision
you can, for the part that you are
able to influence, then simply
watch and wait.

Things are not quite as they might have seemed. Adopt a calm and measured approach, then take another careful look before you make your decision.

Release your emotions, whether
they are positive or negative, and
allow peace and healing
to follow naturally.

Do not judge your own feelings Pisces
– deciding that they are 'good' or 'bad'
is entirely unhelpful. Allow them,
simply, to be as they are.

Pure Pisces intuition allows
you to understand even the unsaid
things. Others flourish under your
guidance. But do not confuse being
a sounding board with
being a doormat.

Ensure you have the right balance
between thought and emotion before
you choose your path – head and
heart are both required
in this situation.

Yes, you can. And you could also
find an easier way than you think. But
that doesn't mean that you should.
Think very carefully about the possible
implications before you make
your next move.

You will find a way Pisces, and
there are plenty of openings you can
flow into. Take the easier route
this time if you can.

It is never too late to accept
an apology or to make one yourself.
Only then can you start moving
forwards again.

Allow all the options this time.
The right one will soon become clear.

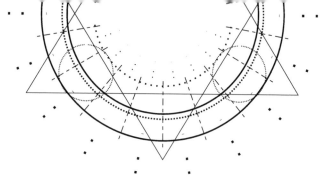

While hard work is never the most appealing option, easy wins can feel less than satisfying. But take the smoothest route this time. Something much more difficult is just around the corner, so that will provide the challenge you crave.

Feed your soul with love and light Pisces. Don't hide away in the shadows or behind impossible aspirations. Love is the answer; make this life as you want it to be, no matter what it takes.

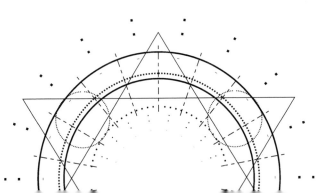

Pisces, your gently compassionate nature can sometimes tip over into sadness or allow you to be easily hurt. Reassure yourself: you are all that you need to be. You are already enough.

Empathy and a willingness to trust are gifts often proffered by a Pisces, but you must be sure to guard your own heart and to protect yourself against sadness and fear or victimization.

Over-thinking will not serve you
Pisces, and, what's more, it's not really
in your nature. Do not devote too
much of your precious time
to this one.

Guard your reservoir of strength carefully Pisces; your energy is a precious resource. If it is looking like this is a disagreement you simply will not be able to avoid, engage only for the shortest possible time and be sure to protect your reserves.

Take the easier route this time if you can Pisces, there are plenty of options. You need to keep a clear head and maintain a steady course to find your way through.

Truly concentrated listening
is a rare and valuable skill. Open
your heart and set preconceived
notions aside. Take the time to truly
hear what others are saying.

The best option will present itself
once you adopt a slightly steadier
approach. Don't allow yourself to be
buffeted by the storm of options;
that will help no one and will send
you into a spin.

Bear all possibilities in mind.
There are several different players to
consider and the path to your goal
is not yet clear.

Rest while you are able to:
something challenging is heading in
your direction.

Your idiosyncratic approach should not be mistaken for flightiness or self-doubt. Include some depth and detail, to reassure others of your commitment and understanding.

Do not allow your desire to avoid harshness and rough edges to turn into an impulse to retreat and hide from the world. Keep at least a toe in the water at all times, otherwise you won't be able to gauge the temperature.

Those born under Pisces are usually more intuitive, often more artistic and generally more musically talented than most other signs... of course, there are always exceptions. If you are struggling to really value your own talents right now, avoid comparison and competition in favour of focusing inwards. That's where the treasure lies.

Caring, faithful and wise, or cautious, fearful and easily hurt? It can be tough out there for more sensitive signs, and protecting your own soul is important. Find gentler ways to engage rather than retreating completely.

Allow the uncertainty you might be feeling to feed into positive plans for the future – invest your time, your knowledge, or perhaps even money into something that will enrich long-term solutions.

Remember that blessings
come in all forms. Take some time
today to appreciate those which have
landed in your lap.

Allowing the chance of
chaos is essential if you are to
ensure a smooth resolution this time.
This storm will settle; watch for a
pattern as it all dies down.

Now is your chance to sink
or swim – don't shy away from a
challenge that seems perfectly tailored
to your talents.

Silence and privacy will be essential if you are to work this one out properly. Wisdom and truth require some quiet to reveal themselves.

Swim out from under that darkness Pisces, it's time to go with the flow. Remember that you are a water sign and, now more than ever, the tide and a clear view of that horizon will show you the direction you should follow.

Empathy flows from you, on a
good day at least, and it is easy for
others to simply enjoy basking in your
glow. Make sure that you are receiving
enough from them by return.

Your generosity and easy charm can attract those looking to heal. Ensure their intentions are good before you allow strangers in. Vanity, greed and competitiveness may prove to be destructive forces.

Allow others an insight into
your thoughts (on the understanding,
of course, that you have every right to
change your mind). Remember to
speak from your heart, with
compassion and understanding.

It can be a shock to others when you suddenly reach empty and your signal fades. Take that all-important time out to reset, then float back in.

Your emotions live close up
under your skin and play a significant
role in the way you live your life and
make your decisions. Not everyone is
quite as emotionally-savvy as you,
remember; some can find it daunting,
or downright perplexing, trying to get
to grip with their own pesky feelings,
let alone those of others.

A dreamy old planet at the best of times, Neptune can lead you into super-sensitivity when the energy flows that way. This will make you much more aware of the feelings and moods of other people – just be careful you don't end up absorbing too much.

You are so in tune with
your surroundings and the
emotions of the people around
you, that it can be difficult knowing
where you end and they begin. Be
mindful you don't become too
entangled in their issues, in case
they drain your energy.

Creative activities, as well as meditation and yoga, are essential to nourish your Piscean spirit and avoid energy blockages. For you, even more than most, it is essential to keep the pathways open.

Neptune slows everything down when it passes through, and as your ruling planet it has a permanent effect on you. You are more present, more emotionally aware and more sensitive than most. Don't waste time trying to be something you are not; use these attributes to your advantage now Pisces.

You are happiest outdoors,
in wild water, serene and surrounded
by nature. Keep this self-knowledge
in your back pocket and draw on it
as your first response when you start
to feel any signs of stress or being
overwhelmed. The waves will
recalibrate you and reset
your soul.

You are utterly devoted
and completely loyal to those
you love Pisces. Be careful that your
dedication doesn't encourage a
tendency to linger longer than you
should in an unproductive or
unhealthy situation; there are some
wounds that cannot be healed.

Try to hold on a little
longer. The time is not yet right,
but it will be soon.

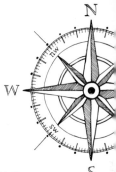

Taking the lead is not always your favourite position Pisces but, with your gifts for help and healing, plenty of others look to you to set an example (whether you are aware of it or not). Show them the way forwards with your trademark compassion and empathy.

Despite your overwhelming
impulse not to fixate on just one thing,
it is important that you are honest
with yourself and others; self-
knowledge and self-expression is
never a weakness.

Your habit is to remain gently, softly ever-present, reassuring in your constancy. But there is nothing more to be gained with this one, staying longer than anyone else will not secure happiness.

There is nothing more dangerous for you than stasis and forced stillness; if you are not able to flow, you risk your energy stagnating and your spirit will suffer, too. In all things, be yourself.

Staying deliberately close or are you stuck? Only you can truly answer this question Pisces. And once you answer it truthfully, you will know what to do.

Deal with issues as they arise Pisces, rather than putting them on the back burner or tumbling to get ahead of yourself. One step at a time, although maybe it wouldn't hurt to pick up the pace a little.

Be mindful of allowing and acknowledging the voices of others as you go about your business. Let them know that they are heard.

Your ability to listen closely and carefully, and to really hear what the other person is saying, is a rare and valuable skill. Use it now.

Look for the easy swim Pisces –
although the big waves may appear
exciting right now, you don't want to
end up out of your depth.

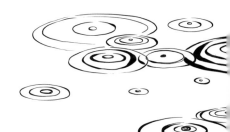

Sometimes just
your presence is enough.

If you are feeling overwhelmed and it seems things might be coming to a head, step forwards rather than backwards Pisces. It's better to meet the wave on your own terms than to passively wait for it to strike.

Active participation is essential Pisces;
resist the urge to stand by and watch.

Grace, sensitivity and gentleness
sit comfortably with you Pisces, and all
around you benefit. Make sure that
you are receiving enough by return to
maintain your personal growth
and to feel nurtured.

Acquisitions and material wealth
are of no value in and of themselves,
and usually you understand this. But
perhaps some shiny bauble has turned
your head this time? Tempting as it
may be, your best step right now
would be to concentrate on enriching
your family or community
in some way.

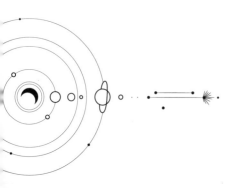

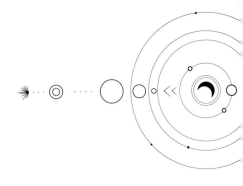

Serenity and calm should be your
aim right now Pisces. Putting chaotic
pockets of your life in order will give
everything a strong push in
the right direction.

Try to include more focus in your practise, whether work or self-improvement. It will bring meaningful gains. Be sure not to push yourself too hard though Pisces; add a little self-love into the mix as well.

When you feel like you could
do with some solidity under your
feet, don't forget that you can lean on
those around you. They will be
flattered that you have noticed how
dependable they are and how
much they care.

Don't be tempted to use power
in the wrong way; join in with everyone
else, connecting with the group and
participating, and you will feel
much happier.

Ensure that you keep your connections at the front of your mind. Your warmth, adaptability and understanding draw people to you; balance these attributes with your intuition and momentum, and you will be sure to make things happen.

It is important that you stay
open and receptive to spontaneity
Pisces – opportunities are sparking
all around you.

A fear of confrontation is no reason to continue with unhealthy behaviours or relationships. Perhaps you are enabling someone else, or perhaps you are not being truthful with yourself. Either way Pisces, both clarity and courage are now required.

Remain open to the possibility of change and embrace all options your curiosity affords you. Keep it clean and straightforward – if there is something you want to know, ask.

If you are feeling the need to surround yourself with softness and ease right now, go with it. Things don't have to be difficult to be worthwhile.

Remember Pisces, although
you love to make sure that everyone
around you is doing fine, you can only
look after them if you take care
of yourself first.

Make the most of your own
identity and your independent
spirit. Even though others rely on
you (sometimes quite a lot), it's
important to remember who you are
without all those connections and
threads running this way and that.
Sometimes you just need to
swim your own strokes.

Temporary disturbances in
your surroundings or social circle
can create ripples that impact your
sense of security and calm. Just go
with the flow and the waters will
settle again soon.

Learn a lesson from your opposite sign Virgo. Letting your thoughts and feelings shimmer on the surface for all to see is not always the best course. Although it may go against the grain, it would be wise to protect yourself a little more than usual.

Although you can see that others may be speaking the truth, it might seem too harsh and unpalatable for you to stomach. Spend some time in dialogue to try and understand what lies beneath the sharpness of their delivery.

When all is harmonious with you Pisces, nothing could be sweeter. Keep your heart and mind open and tune in to that particular resonance of your stars aligning – good things approach.

It is a good time to wriggle free of the obligation-net if you can Pisces, it will do you good to dive straight into a few freedom waves today.

Going with the flow is your usual mode Pisces, but sometimes you might find the direction a little disorienting, perhaps even bewildering. Relinquishing control can be more difficult than you think, but it is essential. Your creativity will benefit.

Do not dismiss new ideas that occur to you; with awareness and a steady observational gaze, you will realize that the universe is supplying you with some pretty heavy deliveries... and they all need to be unpacked. Interesting and inspiring times lie ahead.

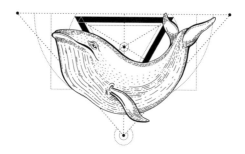

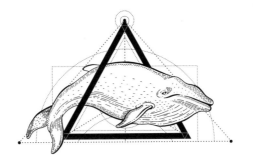

Answers are not always
forthcoming Pisces, and clarity is
not necessarily your main strength.
Opening up to guidance is as much
about allowing and releasing as it is
about trust – have faith and
all will be well.

Be sure about yourself and
what you want from this situation
Pisces; you cannot control each wave
of the tide, but you can make good
use of your intuition and check in
honestly with yourself to be sure you
are following the path of your
own choosing.

Do not allow yourself to be
pressured into situations or actions,
even when others try to persuade you.
You are not a puppet, Pisces.

Perhaps you are susceptible to the influence of a powerful personality right now Pisces. Rather than pushing back, simply flow smoothly and coolly out of their grasp – no need for drama or heavy conversations. Stay true to yourself.

Embrace your entire self Pisces, without fear, judgement or anger, but instead with full knowledge, an open heart and acceptance. You are entirely deserving of complete love.

On the days that feel difficult, when time is sticky and the presence of others can jangle your nerves, take a big step back into some serious self-love and know that you are enough.

When home feels a frazzled place, bubbling with tension and possibly even conflict, find yourself a soul-base within a small, safe area or perhaps even outside somewhere. It is important you have a physical space you can return to, both physically and emotionally.

Remember, if you want to communicate an important message to someone in particular, you need to be speaking a language they will understand.

Dear Pisces: if you feel you
have something to say, don't
hold your tongue. Your contribution
is needed and valuable, and there is
every chance that what you say might
be a great help to someone else,
even if you never know it.
Say your piece.

Maintaining a strong and
healthy energy flow is essential for
you Pisces, especially for keeping that
precious creativity moving through.
Pay close attention to your own needs.

Take part in the conversation
Pisces; now is not the time for
watching from the sidelines. Be ever
mindful of the power and weight
words carry and choose
yours carefully.

Even if events seem to be moving faster than you can keep up with, maintain your own pace and deal with what you can in your own time. If you don't hold your footing, you risk being swept along and losing your sense of direction.

Perhaps you are daunted by the prospect of a difficult situation Pisces. It's easy to lose your sense of self when faced with obstacles, but there is a strong chance that this may not be anywhere near as difficult as you fear, once you actually come to deal with it. In any case, you must engage with it now.

Moving into this next stage
Pisces, it is vital that you are open
with others about your weaknesses
and honest about your concerns. Your
vulnerability might feel risky, but
it is a lot safer than allowing
others to believe that things
are not as they are.

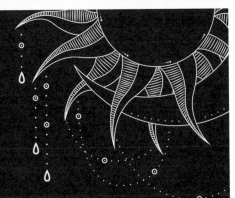

If situations are confused at
the moment, don't feel you need to
expend loads of energy trying to
work it out Pisces. Making sense of
it all might be a task better left to
another day, when everything
is more settled.

Give even greater consideration than usual to the needs of others right now Pisces; there are undercurrents of things unsaid flowing through a particular situation. Don't become sidetracked.

Your Piscean nature doesn't always bow to the tyranny of timekeeping, but you must be respectful of others' time especially at the moment. Don't leave people waiting too long.

Given to flowing freely
like the true water sign you
are Pisces, remember your need
for quiet and solitude when the time
comes to recharge. Super-sensitive
souls need extra rest
and nourishment.

Be sure to check in regularly with your emotions Pisces; not paying attention to them, or even worse bottling them up, can lead to a dangerous pressure-cooker of feelings that may well boil over when it is least convenient.

Balance and connection are
vital to a super-intuitive free spirit
like you Pisces. Holistic harmony and
self-expression must be prioritized and
actively invested in for the sake of
your wellbeing.

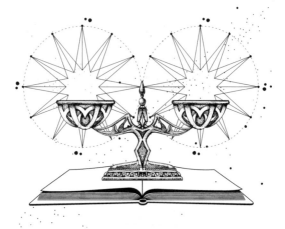

It's important that your communication channels are open and flowing freely Pisces. It might be that you are encountering someone who it seems is trying to block you. Pay attention to both the said and the unsaid and find an easy, gentle way around the problem.

Do not let one individual sway your opinion of your own progress, or even worse, alter your course. Try thinking differently instead Pisces. Address any problems that arise, or potential solutions, with everyone's best interests in mind.

Your powerful Pisces
intuition is a blessing, of course
it is. But sometimes you are so in sync
with others that you feel their feelings
and almost think their thoughts – and
that can be exhausting! Make the most
of your knitted energies at the
moment by moving things forwards
for everyone; others will appreciate
you sharing your momentum.

The behaviour of drama-creators
might be particularly draining right
now Pisces. There is no obligation for
you to engage with or support
whatever is going on.

Good days have been coming your way more often than usual recently... or have you been too busy to notice? Make sure you take some time to see what's going on around you as well as pushing forwards Pisces; it's all too easy to get swept up in events.

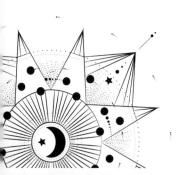

The synergy you feel with
others is a powerful Pisces trait
and the affinity it affords you presents
a chance to expand and deepen your
connections. Relish the opportunities
and enjoy yourself.

Someone from your past appearing unexpectedly in your thoughts or popping up in your life might offer a bridge to new opportunities or different aspects of something you are already interested in. Just don't lose yourself in a dream-past or assume things will be the same as they were: everything changes.

Out of sight doesn't mean out
of mind; your Pisces intuition means
that if someone is in your thoughts
there is a good chance they might be
thinking of you as well. Release any
impulse to hold fast though,
just wait and see.

Your empathy means that
you probably already know that
something is slightly off – a situation,
a new connection or an event or
person you were once sure of. Keep
your eyes open to figure this out.

Circularity may well be in play at the moment Pisces; chasing your tail isn't as silly as it sounds when you remember that the lines between beginnings and endings are often more blurred than you expect.

Just say 'No' Pisces.

Extreme Piscean sensitivity
often results in a need for escapism.
Be careful not to indulge this need to
the point it causes harm to yourself or
others. Keep it occasional.

A huge decision is on the horizon for you Pisces, but with your constantly flowing intuition you are more than up to the challenge. Don't be daunted or start flip-flopping about. Breathe, focus, act.

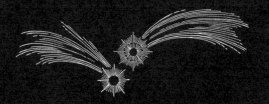

Try to choose the less serious path at the moment Pisces; look for the fun in every opportunity. If there is a chance to enjoy yourself, you should accept it.

There is much strength in vulnerability, everyone has ups and downs, and everyone has their own struggles. Be brave and honest about what you are going through.

A particularly dreamy sign at the best of times Pisces, it can sometimes feel like a struggle to distinguish reality from your vivid imaginings. Truth and fiction may get all mixed up and it might feel almost impossible to find solid footing. Confiding in others will be the first step to feeling a bit more grounded.

Your experiences change you Pisces; with your sensitivity and particular emotional makeup, there is no way around that. But you do not have to be passive, if you engage and pay attention you can use altering circumstances as a chance to reinvent or reposition yourself more favourably.

It's all about movement for you Pisces, and as a water sign, that's no surprise. When communication is flowing freely you are better able to both express and process your own feelings. This makes you less likely to get swept up in someone else's emotional storm, which is a good thing.

Major change can be upsetting,
or stressful, but it can also be an
opportunity to engage with fresh eyes
and renewed creativity. Ringfence
some time to be alone and to think
about the next steps you
would like to make.

Following your intuition is less
of a choice and more of a compulsion
for you Pisces – is there any other way
to live? Well, yes. Stay awake to the
fact that most other people do not
experience or process the world in
the same way you do – our
differences are infinite.

Seeing transformation in others
can be nothing short of inspirational –
perhaps you are now thinking of some
big changes for yourself. Whichever
way you decide to go with this, be
careful you are making your own
decisions for the right reasons, rather
than just because you now prefer
the look of someone else's
order to your own.

Asking expert advice is the
best course of action Pisces; with a
few pointers and a bit of inside
knowledge you might amaze yourself
with how quickly a whole new plan
can come together.

Spending some quality time on yourself is a good idea right now Pisces, and whether that means a holistic treatment, a day off or just a long, uninterrupted rest is up to you. Now is the time to create some downtime and make the most of it.

Don't leap without looking Pisces –
you might find yourself head-down in
a too-small bucket rather than
luxuriating in the waves.

Take the time to set your intentions before you enter into new ventures or space Pisces. Be very clear in your own mind about what you are bringing, how you will engage and what you hope to achieve (whether it is for yourself or for others). Clarity makes all the difference.

You're not usually given to guilt Pisces, but right now it might be difficult to escape the nagging doubt that perhaps there is something you could have done better. Deal with it if you can, but move on if you can't. Don't allow yourself to be manipulated.

Do not feed into anyone else's drama Pisces – you are perfectly entitled to refuse to participate.

Slip into the water Pisces; as the fish of the zodiac, it's important you return to your element as often as possible. Not everyone will understand the pull exerted by the waves, but you must pay attention to your soul.

Keeping up with work issues
and professional obligations should
take priority right now Pisces; all else
will have to wait while you fulfil
your duties.

With your intuition pitch perfect
at the moment Pisces, you won't
set a foot wrong as long as you pay
attention to your instincts. Don't
allow the game-plans of others
to throw you off-course.

Investigate the facts, collect the
data, do the spreadsheets – of course,
all of that is important and necessary
groundwork. But ultimately it will be
your heart making this decision,
not your head. Understand
that and allow it.

Tuning into your inner self will mean that you are already listening when important answers to critical issues arise. Do not be tempted to ignore your heart's voice.

Over-dominant people might disproportionately skew the dynamics for you at the moment Pisces. If you have the option, keep out of their orbit for the time being.

Take this opportunity to sharpen up your self-care regime and boost your energy with more focus on healthy living Pisces. There's always room for improvement.

Competitive urges may arise in
your contact group Pisces; retreat into
laughter if it all starts to feel too much.
Keep it light and don't cross any lines.

Time to prioritize your tasks
Pisces – you can't possibly tick
everything off all at once, so focus on
the most urgent and put the rest into
a holding pattern. You will get
to them eventually.

Hold onto your integrity Pisces;
with such a lot going on right now
it is important to maintain your
own equilibrium and behave
according to your own rules.

Feeling a bit haunted by something you should have/could have done differently Pisces? Make a swift, clean apology or reach out a hand while there is still time. Don't dwell on it, deal with it.

If you've woken up with an extra spring in your step today, make the most of that energy to work through some of the backlog that's been building up. Alternatively, if you are feeling more still than usual, take the time to stop and think things through. Both approaches will be massively beneficial right now.

If communications seem difficult at the moment, perhaps you are not considering the preconceptions of your intended recipient. Possibly the way you are framing your ideas simply isn't resonating with them. Step back and try to see this from their perspective – what are you missing?

Stand outside your usual approach today Pisces. Engagement will not be as effective as you hope. Spend some time watching and learning instead.

When uncertainty is strong, rely on your creative strengths to navigate through the fog. You don't need to make sense of everything Pisces, just be sure you have a sense of direction and purpose.

What you consider pragmatism others may well be reading as self-centredness Pisces. Tune in to your legendary empathy to better understand how they are hearing you.

Your shape-shifting Pisces nature is about to come in handy. With so many different types suddenly in the mix, your ability to instinctively understand and respond to each person's needs will be tremendously valuable and save a whole lot of time.

Fantasist or imaginative genius? Probably it depends who you ask... But one thing is for sure: as long as you are using your creativity to deepen your engagement rather than running away, you are onto a certain winner.

In times of stress or generally feeling like things are not quite in sync, return to the water Pisces. There, everything comes back together for you.

Self-expression can take many forms
Pisces; be sure to find the one that
works for you as such an outlet will be
essential in retaining your balance.

Your intuitive and emotional
style can sometimes seem a little
'spooky' to the less-switched-on signs.
Cut them some slack and adopt a
warm and disarming approach
when dealing with them.

Flick your tail and head back the way
you came Pisces – you've taken a
wrong turn somewhere upstream.

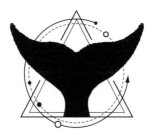

Big changes are on their way
Pisces – remain alert to possibilities
and opportunities that will arise.

Misunderstandings may occur because of a disconnect or an enforced distance Pisces. Act quickly to close the gap and repair any resulting rift.

Firing up your creativity will
place you in a strong position to
expand your experience and
understanding. Opportunities often
arise from unexpected sources.

Learning is never wasted Pisces.
If you have been toying with the idea
of further experience or new training,
remember that there is no time like the
present. Make it happen.

Artistic leanings will open new doors for you Pisces. Go with the flow to see where it takes you.

Boost your blood flow and your
brain with a fresh addition to your
exercise regime Pisces. It doesn't have
to be anything huge, even a small
change will make a difference
to how you feel.

Relish the calm waters when
you find them Pisces. Do not overlook
those who offer you quiet support and
understanding in favour of others who
are all about excitement and thrilling
waves. People who hold space for you,
and simply allow you to be,
should be treasured.

In a rut of routine or a tangle of thoughts Pisces? Pull yourself out by starting to make small changes at first – you will be amazed at their cumulative effects in a relatively short time.

New colours, books, experiences, styles or flavours will feed your soul and expand positivity in all parts of your life. Stand tall, speak clearly, own your space.

You have many choices to
make at the moment Pisces, but
one is particularly important. Bridging
a certain gap will alter the direction
your future path will follow.

Courage is vital right now Pisces, and circling your thoughts will not help you. Grasp the opportunity when it arises and say what needs to be said.

Reject fearful thoughts of what might happen and simply aim towards your goal of creating the outcome you desire. It really is that simple Pisces.

Chasing this one upstream might
well be worth the effort Pisces.
There will be many twists and turns to
follow, but the prize will be significant.

Time spent alone will be increasingly valuable at the moment Pisces. You need to think through some problems that have been presenting recently; most importantly, a shift in energy and comfort levels in a particular relationship. Time to sort this out.